MW01247867

INTERNALIZING
the
WORD
G*of*OD

A PROVEN STEP-BY-STEP PROCESS
TO SCRIPTURE MEMORY

MIKE HARRISON

ISBN 979-8-89309-183-0 (Paperback)
ISBN 979-8-89309-184-7 (Digital)

Covenant Books
11661 Hwy 707
Murrells Inlet, SC 29576
www.covenantbooks.com

If I were to tell you right now, "I will give you $1000 for every Bible verse you can memorize in seven days," without a doubt, I am certain that you would drop everything in your schedule and focus on this once-in-a-lifetime opportunity. Would it be difficult? Yes. Would it be worth your time, your attention, your sacrifice? Absolutely.

Enthusiasm and good intentions do not make up for preparation and objective effort. The proof of your desire to know and recall God's Word directly corresponds to your effort. This is James's exhortation when he boldly confronts the idea of faith and deeds. He says, "S how me your faith by what you do" (James 2:18). He references Abraham, whose faith was made complete by what he did. His faith and his actions were working together (James 2:14–26). The fact that you are still reading this is an indicator of your desire. There is a seed, so rejoice, and together, let us prepare the ground so that we can plant this seed deep into nutrient-rich soil.

What does it mean to memorize the Word of God? The goal here is not to just "memorize" for the sake of memorization. This is not like cramming at the last minute before an exam so that you pass the test. This is so much more than that. I am proposing that you *internalize* God's Word, placing it deep into your heart where it will consistently produce fruit, providing comfort and peace, hope and assurance and encouragement, equipping the followers of Jesus Christ with the capacity to defend their faith and exhort fellow Christians. To internalize something requires will and desire, accompanied by a process and a plan. Assimilation is the process of internalization. Absorbing, understanding, applying, and living God's Word results in a changed life.

Before we dive into the nuts or bolts of internalizing the Word of God, we must first make certain that we have planted this precious seed in fertile soil. After the soil prep, we will then examine and look at the "why" of memorizing scripture. Only then can we learn how to internalize God's Word in our hearts.

PREPARING THE SOIL

In the Parable of the Soils (Matthew 13:1–23, Mark 4:1–20, Luke 8:4–15), the growth and maturation of the seed is dependent upon not only the soil in which it is planted but also the nurturing of the seed that comes from watering, feeding, protecting, and caring for it. Jesus references one kind of seed planted in four different soils. The seeds are the same, but where they have been planted directly influences the growth and maturation of the seed. There is only one reason to plant a seed, and that is to have it grow and produce fruit. A farmer plants seeds with the expectation of harvesting a future crop. However, before he plants the seeds, he carefully and painstakingly prepares the soil to receive the seeds, providing the best-case scenario for them to grow. He prepares the soil. He plants the seed. He then carefully cultivates and irrigates his field, filled with the expectation of a bountiful harvest.

Indulge me for a minute as we dig a little deeper in our examination of the seed. Let us agree together that Jesus Christ was the promised Seed that was *conveyed* to Adam in Genesis 3:15, and *confirmed* to Abraham in Genesis 12,15, and 22 and to David in 2 Samuel 7, and *completed* in Jesus Christ in John 12:23, Galatians 3:15–16, and many other biblical references to Jesus as the Seed.

As Paul famously said in Galatians 3:15, "Let me take an example from everyday life." I would also like to give you an example from everyday life. For a seed to grow, it must first die. This example of everyday life has powerful implications and directly correlates with our own spiritual growth and sanctification in Christ. Jesus Christ, being the promised Seed, had to die to give us life. Understand this: as sin entered the world through one man, so also death came to all men. But life was given through the death, burial, and resurrection of one man, Jesus Christ. Those who surrender to and humbly accept by faith Jesus Christ as their Lord and Savior receive the Holy Spirit and are grafted into the family of God (Romans 5). The Seed had to die to produce life. In John 10:10, Jesus declares that He came to give life, not only life but abundant life.

Do you want to live an abundant life? Just like Jesus Christ had to die, we, too, must die to receive life. Not die physically, as Jesus did, but to die to ourselves. The apostle Paul died to himself on the road to Damascus (Acts 9). His life drastically changed following his "Mack truck encounter" with Jesus Christ. In Galatians 2:20, Paul said, "I have been crucified with Christ and I no longer live, but Christ lives in me." In Colossians 3:3, Paul, speaking to Christians, said, "For you died and your life is now hidden with Christ in God." Further, Paul speaks of the cross of Christ. In 1 Corinthians 15:1–4, Paul unapologetically declares that Jesus Christ died for our sins. He was buried, and raised on the third day according to the Scriptures. His death brought us life. The Cross of Christ represents God's love, mercy, forgiveness, and grace. The message of the cross, which is the Gospel of Jesus Christ, is the power of God to those who are being saved (1 Corinthians 1:18).

There is the point I am trying to drive home. The desire to memorize Scripture must be born from a heart that has first been totally surrendered to Jesus Christ.

If you have not surrendered to the Lord Jesus Christ, confessed, and repented from your sins and have accepted by faith that Jesus Christ died for your sins, may I humbly invite you to do so right now. Maybe you gave your life to him years ago and have wandered from the faith? Maybe you are unsure of whether your decision was authentic. Remove any doubt right now, get on your knees, confess your sins, and ask Jesus to become the Lord of your life. Romans 10:13 says, "Everyone who calls on the name of the Lord will be saved." That is a promise. "For it is with your heart that you believe and are justified, and it is with your mouth that you confess and are saved" (Romans 10:9–10). Do not let another second pass you by. The gift of salvation is under the Christmas tree with your name on it. There is an urgency here for Jesus is going to return like a thief in the night (1 Thessalonians 5). He said himself in Mark 13:33, "You do not know when that time will come." Friends, "Repent for the Kingdom of heaven is near" (Matthew 4:17). "Now is the time of God's favor, now is the day of salvation" (2 Corinthians 6:1).

Take note: justification is what God does for us. Sanctification is what God does through us on this road to Glorification, which occurs when we die and get to spend eternity in heaven with Him. Those who are authentic followers of Christ are given, at the point of salvation, the promised Holy Spirit who takes up permanent residency in our lives. Paul gloriously exhorts us in Ephesians 1:13–14, "And you also were included in Christ when you heard the message of truth, the gospel of your salvation. When you believed, you were marked in Him with a seal, the promised Holy Spirit, who is a deposit guaranteeing our inheritance until the redemption of those who are God's possession—to the praise of His glory." God has sent the Holy Spirit into our hearts (Galatians 4:6), and it is our guaranteed admittance into heaven (2 Corinthians 1:22).

It is the gracious gift of God that we are sealed with the Holy Spirit, whereby He demonstrates the authenticity of our relationship with Him and His authority, ownership, and commitment to us.

In ancient times, a king would bestow his royal seal that represented his trust and manifestation of his royal authority, approval, and protection. It was a big deal to have the king's seal. In modern times, this would be like possessing a full-access backstage pass at a concert, festival, or other venue. The Holy Spirit moves into one's heart and becomes the tenant who stays there forever. It is the work of the Holy Spirit that enables us to understand why we are to internalize the Word of God and implement how. Now that the "seed" has been planted, let us now define the why.

WHY INTERNALIZE AND ASSIMILATE THE WORD OF GOD?

Have you ever heard someone make a statement claiming it to be valid, authentic, and reliable truth, but something made you doubt or question the accuracy of their claim? The appropriate response to any declaration ought to be, "Where is that written in the Bible?" Is the statement objective or subjective? John said in 1 John 4:1, "Do not believe every spirit, but test the spirits to see whether they are from God." Paul exhorted the Thessalonians to "test everything" (1 Thessalonians 5:21). Finally, Jesus commanded us to "Be on guard! Be Alert!" (Mark 13:33) so that no one deceives you. Why am I stressing this? Christians are constantly being exposed to false teachings and heresy. Consequently, we should consider the source and hold every truth claim up to the true, living, and active Word of God. Deception, misinformation, and false teaching are spreading like wildfire today, much of that due to how quickly information spreads over the internet. If you recall, the first sin ever committed was one born of a lie (Genesis 3:1). As a result, Christians must thoroughly know the truth so that they can quickly spot the lie.

The Federal Agents who are tasked with the detection of counterfeit currency do not waste their time studying the counterfeit bills that agents in the field find. No, they painstakingly observe and study the genuine bills. They touch them, and they look at them from every angle; they even hold them to the light and look through them. They memorize the characteristics and unique features of the original so that when they see a fake bill, they can quickly identify it as counterfeit. Christians must take the same disciplined approach toward the Word of God. Jesus said in John 8:31–32, "The truth will set you free." There is a powerful, unlocked, and unchained freedom that comes from knowing the truth.

One of my favorite sections in the Bible is 1 Peter 4:7–13. Here is the context. In this letter, Peter instructs and exhorts followers of Jesus how to live for God. He starts off by identifying the living hope that comes from the resurrection of Jesus Christ. Then he exhorts us to be holy because Jesus is holy, to rid ourselves of hypocrisy, and to crave pure spiritual milk. Next, Peter speaks of suffering for Christ and living for God. He encourages us to serve others using the gift that God has given us. He then says in verse 11, "If anyone speaks, he should do so as one speaking the very words of God." This is a powerful and emphatic encouragement to say what God has said.

The Bible says that faith comes through hearing the Word of God (Romans 10:17). It is God who does the saving and justifying. As His faithful followers, we become seed planters, but it is He who makes the seeds grow. What am I saying? Words matter! What we say and how we say it matters a great deal. Therefore, if we all can agree that Peter's exhortation to "speak the very words of God" is to all Christians, then we must know His Word and have it stored in our heads and in our hearts so that we might coherently and confidently speak His Word.

Let us take time to see what the Word of God has to say about internalizing the Holy Scriptures.

MIKE HARRISON

Let me first qualify that this will not be an exhaustive list or response to a very expansive topic.

The Word of God instructs those marked with the promised seal of the Holy Spirit to understand, meditate on, and obey His Word. Let us go to the Word and see what it says. We will examine both Old and New Testament references that support this claim. Remember that the appropriate response to any assertion is, "Where is it written?"

OLD TESTAMENT
REFERENCES

In the fourth book of the Bible, Deuteronomy, God sets His people apart from the other nations and peoples. The Israelites had been rescued from slavery and were about to enter the promised land. He instructs them to observe His commands, which will give them strength. That is, God's Word gives us strength. Then in Deuteronomy 11:18, God instructs His people, through Moses, to, "Fix these words of mine in your hearts and minds; tie them as symbols on your hands and bind them on your foreheads." He goes on to say, "Teach them and talk about them." This exhortation and command also applies to the followers of Christ today. We are to hold up His Word as the authority that will govern our thoughts and our actions. Psalm 19:14 says, "May the Words of my mouth and the meditation of my heart be pleasing in Your sight, O Lord, my Rock, and my Redeemer."

As we follow the great exodus narrative, we are introduced to Joshua, to whom God passed the torch of leadership following the death of Moses. He is the one who led the Israelites into the promised land by crossing the Jordan and onto Jericho to take possession of the land. In Joshua 1:8, God exhorted Joshua, "Do not let this Book of the Law depart from your mouth; meditate on it day and night, so that you may be careful to do everything that is written in it." Again, this command is for us to consider and embrace. Joshua only had the *Torah*, the first five books of the Bible. We have the whole story, all sixty-six books. We know how God's redemptive love story unfolds and culminates on the cross of Calvary, and in that message is the power of God (1 Corinthians 1:18). We are not justified by obeying God's commands. We are saved by grace through faith in Christ and not by works (Ephesians 2:8–10). God commanded Joshua to meditate on His Word, that is, to understand it, know it, and recall it, so that he would be careful to "do" (that is to obey) everything written in it. We are encouraged to apply this virtue and realize that following it, obeying it, and applying it makes us participants in the sanctification process of our lives.

Who does not want to be blessed? I don't think anyone would choose not to be blessed and instead desire to be cursed. The book of Psalms is the longest book in the Bible, and the first three verses offer us a glimpse into God's desire for us to value His Word. It says, "Blessed is the man who does not walk in the council of the wicked or stand in the way of sinners or sit in the seat of mockers. But his delight is in the law of the Lord, and on His law, he meditates day and night. He is like a tree planted by streams of water, which yields its fruit in season and whose leaf does not wither. Whatever he does prospers" (Psalm 1:1–3). There is so much to unpack in these verses. Let us focus on the man who is blessed because his delight is in the law of the Lord, on which he meditates day and night. The present-day definition of meditation refers to emptying your mind. This is the antithesis of the original meaning and intent of the word meditation. In this context, within the Hebrew language, to meditate is to ponder or imagine. Consider pondering the Word of God, keeping it stored in your head and heart. Think about it day and night. This powerful charge has amazing promises that are unlocked for those who choose to do it.

Psalm 119 is the longest chapter in the Bible, and it has 176 verses and all but five reference God's laws, statutes, precepts, and commands. The author reiterates the value, provision, and preserving power of God's Word in our sanctification. In 119:11, the author offers a powerful promise for all believers in Christ. He says, "I have hidden Your word in my heart that I may not sin against You." When God exposed and revealed this verse to me several years ago, it ignited the now raging fire and burning desire inside of me to internalize His Word. To store it deep in my heart and to teach others how to do it. When we follow this command, there are countless benefits, and one of them is sinning less. God hates sin, and when His Word is given full backstage access to our thoughts, lives, and hearts, we begin to view sin the way He views sin. In Romans 12:1–2, Paul lays down a strong urging and exhortation to be "transformed by the renewing of your mind" because when we do that then "God's good pleasing and perfect will is tested and approved."

A verse that is often referenced is Isaiah 55:8, which says, "For My thoughts are not your thoughts, neither are your ways My ways declares the Lord."

The minor prophet Amos, in his self-titled book in the Old Testament, dovetails this verse beautifully in 4:13, where he says, "He who forms the mountains, creates the wind, and reveals His thoughts to man, He who turns dawn to darkness and treads the high places of the earth—the Lord God Almighty is His name." Did you see that? These verses do not contradict each other. They wonderfully and supernaturally give us hope in the mysteries of God. He reveals His thoughts to us in the Word of God, the Holy Bible. How exciting is that?

Finally, though, there are many more references in the Old Testament that support the question, "Why internalize the Word of God?" In the book of Proverbs, which is so famously referred to as the *Book of Wisdom*, the author asserts in 30:5, "Every Word of God is flawless, He is shield to those who take refuge in Him." God's shielding and protecting sovereign power covers those who choose to feed on His Word. Jeremiah said it this way, "When your words came, I ate them; they were my joy and my heart's delight" (Jeremiah 15:16). God's Word, the holy inerrant Bible, is flawless. It is perfect! He becomes a shield to those who intentionally put His Word on and store it in their hearts.

Remember those federal agents who spend their time studying genuine currency so that they may quickly spot the counterfeit? Why internalize God's truth? So that we can spot the counterfeits.

NEW TESTAMENT
REFERENCES

Again, I must reiterate that this list only scratches the surface as we unearth the answer to the claim that we should store up God's Word in our heads and hearts. Let us start in Matthew and look at the life of Jesus Christ, the Messiah, who gives us a very practical example of what storing up the Word of God in our hearts looks like.

In the first chapters of the Gospel of Matthew, we find Jesus being baptized by John the Baptist. Following His baptism, He is immediately led by the Holy Spirit into the wilderness to be tempted by the devil himself. We are not going to unpack this narrative thoroughly and exhaustively. This will be a broad, thirty-thousand-foot overview. We learn that after forty straight days of fasting, Jesus is then tempted. Do not let that fact go unnoticed. Jesus was tempted though without sin (Hebrews 4:15). Though He was fully God, He was also fully man and was tempted. He was obviously hungry and thirsty. He was weak and vulnerable. The devil, who knew that Jesus was physically depleted, tempted Him with food. He challenges and mocks Jesus, saying, "If you are the Son of God, tell these stones to become bread" (Matthew 4:3). How does our Lord respond? He immediately recites scripture from Deuteronomy 8:3 and says, "It is written: Man does not live on bread alone but on every word that comes from the mouth of God." Though lengthy sermons could be preached on this single verse, let me offer two takeaways.

First, Jesus boldly declares that our source of life and our very sustenance ought to be the Word of God. Jesus later says that He is the way, the truth, and the life and that if we go to Him, we will never go hungry or be thirsty (John 14:6 and 6:35). Second, Jesus gives us the blueprints for life in how we should respond when we are tempted to sin. We are instructed to counter every flaming arrow of attack with the sword of the Spirit, which is the Word of God (Ephesians 6:10–18)

There is no more powerful answer and reason for the exhortation for Christians to memorize, internalize, and assimilate the very Words of God in our heads and hearts. Nevertheless, for the sake of leaving no stone unturned, let us look at some more examples.

In John 14, Jesus spoke of His departure from this world and promised to send His Holy Spirit to comfort and guide the apostles in the days ahead. He followed those words with an analogy that we find in John 15. Here, He referred to Himself as the True Vine and His followers as the branches on the Vine. This is a powerful picture that our Lord wants us to understand. Branches grow out of the vine, not the other way around. Jesus said that apart from Him, we can do nothing. The branch cannot say to the vine, I don't need you. Jesus then implores us to remain in Him and to have His Words remain or abide in us. The Greek word used in this passage, *měnō*, means to abide, to stay, and to dwell in. Jesus is charging His disciples (Christians) to store up His Words in our hearts.

Consider the life of the apostle Paul before his name was changed. This name change was representative of his life being changed by an encounter with Christ on the road to Damascus (Acts 9). At that time, he was Saul, a devout Pharisee on a mission to destroy the Church. Jesus met him right where he was, in his sin. Jesus rescued and redeemed him and changed his life forever. Jesus has done the same for you and me. Paul's life mission became the spreading of the Good News of salvation by grace, through faith in Christ, and not by works (Ephesians 2:8–9).

In his letter to the Colossians, Paul urges us to "Let the Word of Christ dwell in you richly..." (Colossians 3:16). There is that word dwell again. Paul is reiterating Jesus's exhortation from John 15. It is a choice that we make. When someone comes to your door, you have the choice of whether to let them into your house or not. Paul is calling us to "let the Word in." Make the choice, say yes, and invite the Word to dwell in you and be governed by His Word, His Truth. We are sanctified by His Truth; His Word is Truth (John 17:17). Look at how Paul emphasizes this charge. Not only are we encouraged to let the Word dwell in us, but we are to do it "richly." That means abundantly, exclusively, and completely. Then, we are to give His Word full access to every room in our house. He decides what stays and what goes. His Word is granted the rightful place of complete authority. We subsequently "do what it says" (James 1:22–25). In those passages in James, he tells us that we are blessed when we look intently into the perfect law that gives freedom. A powerful exhortation to closely examine, like one looking through a microscope, we discover the beauty and freedom that comes from obeying.

His Word can be likened to a snowflake. I live in Truckee, California, where we average over 200 inches of snowfall per year. It is such a magical and peaceful thing to watch the snow gently fall from the sky to the ground. There's a sense of peace and calmness that is indescribable. If you were to bend down and examine each snowflake under a microscope, you would see so much more. The uniqueness and beauty of each individual snowflake is just one example of the uniqueness of God's beautiful creation.

The apostle Paul was a mentor to Timothy. Timothy had likely come to faith on Paul's first missionary journey to Derby and Lystra. Paul referred to Timothy as his "true son of faith" (1 Timothy 1:2). Though Timothy was Greek, Paul took this young man under his wing and discipled him in the faith. In 2 Timothy 3:16–17, Paul confidently asserts, "All scripture is God-breathed and is useful for teaching, rebuking, correcting, and training in righteousness." Paul lists virtues that spring forth from studying, knowing, and obeying the scriptures. Entire books are written on just these two verses. The main point that I am driving home here is that for those characteristics to become part of your spiritual DNA, you must discipline yourself to study, meditate, and internalize the Word of God. Scripture is vital for our sanctification; therefore, we need to know it and "fix these words in our hearts and minds; tie them as symbols on our hands and bind them on our foreheads" (Deuteronomy 11:18). Paul concludes his point, saying, "So that the man of God may be thoroughly equipped for every good work" (2 Timothy 3:17). Thoroughly equipped is like a soldier who has successfully completed all his training. He has demonstrated proficiency, he has been tested and approved, and he is ready for war. We, too, are in and at war. We must be thoroughly equipped and ready for the battle.

Finally, let's look at one more supportive scripture to answer the "why"? The Apostle Peter, in his first self-titled letter, encourages us to be holy and endure hardship while we suffer for the Lord. We are encouraged to cling to the "living hope" that was given through the resurrection of Jesus Christ from the dead (1 Peter 1:3). Then he charges Christians to be prepared and ready to answer when asked, "Why do we have hope?" We ought to look and live differently than the world. We are to suffer hardships and persecutions faithfully and confidently. So when we are asked about the hope that we are emitting, we are prepared with an answer. Peter instructs us to first, "In our hearts, set apart Christ as Lord." Then after having called upon the Lord for salvation, we are to "always be prepared." Think of always turning on the light switch and never turning it off. It is always, all the time, on. Being ready for people to ask and be prepared to "answer with gentleness and respect." What is the reason for your hope? Can you succinctly and confidently answer that question with Scripture? To have those answers ready, they must be neatly stored, stacked, and organized in the pantry of our minds.

> The Word of God ought to be neatly stacked and stored in the pantry of our minds. (John Piper)

Before we get into the "how" let me offer an illustration that will hopefully solidify your resolve in this matter; we all are very aware of how our phones and computers work when we are online and connected to the internet. If our connection is secure, we can download information at will. However, when the signal is down and connection has been lost with the server, the dreadful warning prompt appears on the screen, "You are offline." We have all experienced it and know what it exactly means. The source of new available information is no longer available. We only have access to what we previously downloaded and saved to our hard drive.

Why memorize, internalize, and assimilate the Word of God? So that we have it ready when working "offline."

Currently, at this present moment, the United States is a free country where we have religious freedom. The Bible is readily accessible and legal to own, read, and study. However, there may come a time when that is not the case. If that happens, those who have verses, sections, chapters, or books memorized will be far more equipped to resist and endure persecution while exhorting fellow believers with the Word of God.

Are you ready to learn how? Buckle up; here we go.

HOW TO INTERNALIZE AND ASSIMILATE THE WORD OF GOD IN YOUR HEART?

Bible memorization is absolutely
fundamental to spiritual
formation. If I had to choose
between all the disciplines of
the spiritual life, I would choose
Bible memorization, because it
is a fundamental way of filling
our minds with what it needs.
—Dallas Willard

Filling our minds with what they "need." We are surrounded by deception, misinformation, and false teaching. Our minds must have and continue to be fed on the truth to keep the sanctifying engines of our lives running smoothly, efficiently, and effectively.

The manufactured excuses are widespread. Oftentimes, when I share scripture while exhorting and encouraging others to internalize God's Word in their hearts, the immediate response is something like this, "I used to memorize scripture, but now I just don't have the time, or I'm just not good at it, or I have tried, but I cannot seem to do it." Notice how all the responses start with "I." Rote memorization is not an exhortation. This type of memorization is based solely on repetition, though that is a technique that I utilize. What I am advocating is internalizing and assimilating His Word in your heart. It is creating a well-worn path between head knowledge and planting it deep into our hearts. Repetition accelerates this process.

It is not just reciting it; it is knowing the context and understanding the author's original audience, tone, intent, and meaning. It is meditating on the scriptures and praying the scriptures. It is living it daily. It is not just head knowledge that rote memorization enlists. It is one step further; it is head knowledge transferred to the heart. Become the Federal Agent tasked with identifying false teachings and deception that oppose the truth of the Gospel and the Word of God.

Psalm 119:11 says, "I have hidden Your word in my heart that I may not sin against You." This is supernatural and cannot be accomplished on our own. We need the Holy Spirit's divine intervention and power. Please do not attempt to implement this discipline in your life without the Holy Spirit's power.

Step 1: Pray

Ask the Lord to equip you. Ask the Holy Spirit to take the helm of your ship and not only your life but your desire to internalize His Word. Pray a prayer like this, "Lord, your Word says to keep Your commands, to meditate on them day and night, to hide Your words in my heart. Please help me, equip, and guide me to internalize Your word. Lord, I have the desire, but I just don't know where to start. Help me."

Remember Jesus's words: "Apart from Me you can do nothing" and "If you remain in Me and My words remain in you, ask whatever you wish, and it will be given to you" (John 15:1–8). This is not prosperity gospel! If we remain in Jesus and keep his words, then what we ask for will be in direct alignment with His will, which is good, pleasing, and perfect (Romans 12:1–2).

Let us go back to the hypothetical offer of $1000 for each verse you memorize. Desire alone is not going to net you any cash. If, at the end of the week, you tell me, "I don't know any new verses, but I can tell you that I really wanted to memorize a lot of verses." I cannot emphasize enough that your "good intentions" are not enough and will not render the desired result. This principle is true in life and in this scriptural discipline.

Psalm 119:173 says, "May Your hand be ready to help me for I have chosen Your precepts." The answer to "Why memorize scripture?" has been thoroughly answered. As we unveil the "how," keep in mind the answers we discussed to the "why." You have decided, you have made a choice, to ask the Lord to equip you with the desire and capacity to internalize His Word. "Lord, may Your hand be ready to help me, help me be successful in this endeavor, help me identify and remove all distractions, please help me."

Prayer is first, and prayer is ongoing and never ceases. 1 Thessalonians 5:17 says, "Pray continually."

The enemy will manufacture roadblocks and detours to get you off the path of scripture memory. Friends, he does not want you to download online to be prepared and ready offline. He knows how powerfully effective and useful the Word of God is. Therefore, he will elicit and hold back no punches to distract and deceive us. Therefore, prayer and constant communication with our Father are vital to your success in this objective. But there is work to be done. It is not going to be easy, but it will be worth the disciplined approach and effort.

Step 2: Make a Goal

Many years ago, I used to be a competitive ultra-endurance athlete competing in twenty-four-hour solo mountain bike races. After I quit racing, I became a coach in hopes of helping other athletes accomplish their personal goals in cycling. As a coach, one of the first questions I would ask prospective clients was, "What do you hope to achieve or expect out of hiring me as your coach?" This question was meant to challenge the athlete to create clear, concise, difficult, yet achievable goals. This principle ought to be applied to approaching scripture memorization. On a broader scale, setting goals should play an important role in your life as a whole.

Have you ever heard the expression "Bad habits are hard to break"? I would submit that it goes both ways and would change that expression to say, "Habits are hard to break, both good and bad." We could go deep into the rabbit hole talking about our neuroanatomy to explain how habits are created. Allow me for a second to reference two scientific terms that help define this process. Neuroplasticity is a term that refers to the capacity of the brain to change and rewire itself in response to the stimulation from learning and experience. Neurogenesis is the ability to create new neurons and connections between neurons. This is what is happening in the brain when it comes to forming habits. God has so wonderfully designed our brains to work this way. The free will that God has given us allows us to choose what neurons we create. Thus, good or bad habits are based on what we learn and experience.

Another familiar idiom says, "Practice makes perfect." I dislike this one, too, and prefer saying, "Practice makes progress." There is only One who is perfect, and his name is Jesus Christ. Consider this order of operation or sequence: Practice makes progress, and progress creates momentum. What is momentum? Momentum is mass in motion. It is directly proportional to an object's mass and velocity. Wait, I thought we were talking about goal setting. Now we are talking about physics and neuroanatomy. Indulge me, if you will, with this illustration:

Let us say you want to get better at running. We all know that just wanting to run longer and faster is not going to get you there. You actually have to lace up your shoes and run. You have to practice. Like anything in life, if you want to improve to become more skilled and proficient, you have to train, rehearse, and repeat the "thing" you want to develop. This is where we activate neurogenesis, creating a new pathway (through learning and experience) toward adaptation and conversion. This develops habit forming, which leads toward an instinctive nature. Thus making something "second nature." Practice makes progress, and progress over time leads to momentum. Momentum grows exponentially as more mass is applied toward reaching maximum velocity. Put it this way, a thirty-ton logging truck traveling down the highway at one hundred miles per hour is significantly harder to stop than a Honda Civic going five miles per hour.

When it comes to the desire to internalize the Word of God in our hearts, we have to utilize our brains in the way God created them. This is where science and faith go hand in hand. It is a choice we get to make when we decide to highly value the Word of God and treasure it in our hearts. Through practice, which we will thoroughly discuss in Step 3, we are essentially activating neurogenesis to be transformed by the Word of God. As mentioned earlier in Romans 12:1–2, "Do not conform any longer to the pattern of this world but be transformed by the renewing of your mind." The renewing of our minds is the spiritual definition of neurogenesis and neuroplasticity.

A close friend of mine named Dave P., who discipled me for a time, had the ability to recite, quote, and reference scripture all the time. He was able to weave scripture into almost any conversation. I was fascinated by his ability to recall the Word of God. That fascination turned into motivation. I wanted to be able to recall scripture like Dave. His example was not just being able to recall scripture, and it was clear and evident in the way he lived that he highly valued the Word and lived it. There was a clear, well-worn path between head knowledge and where it was firmly stored in his heart. It was the way he lived his life, coupled with his ability to recite scripture, that I wanted to emulate. The "seed" of desire was born in my heart.

Back in the days when I was logging countless miles training for bike races, I would frequently train on the road with other cyclists, and we would ride in a group for hours. Interval training was a training strategy whereby we would take turns riding in the front of the group (peloton) and put forth an all-out effort up to exhaustion. This is called riding in a paceline. When the interval period ended, which was not long because of the harder the effort, you would pull to the side and soft pedal to the back of the peloton, allowing someone else to take a turn at the front. Yes, there is a point to this long story. When the lead cyclist, who had just finished his interval at the front, slipped to the rear of the pack, the reason he was able to stay with the peloton after his effort was because of a concept called drafting. Drafting occurs when a cyclist moves into an area of low pressure behind another cyclist, reducing the wind resistance and the amount of energy required to pedal.

In 1 Corinthians 11:1, Paul boldly asserts, "Follow my example, as I follow the example of Christ." Paul was a leader worth following because his life changed on the road to Damascus, and he never looked back. He had unashamedly and unapologetically surrendered to Jesus Christ, and his life consistently confirmed this decision. Jesus Christ is the ultimate example for us to follow. God has also given us examples in our present day of men and women who lead in such a way, creating the wake to follow. We do not follow Paul or Dave, and we follow Jesus.

Step 3: Devise a Plan

Consider building a house from the ground up. There are so many painstaking steps that must be followed and completed in a specific order for a house to be built. There is an order of operation. The designer and architect are the first resources that start this arduous relay race. The blueprints must be drawn up first. You cannot just start throwing the sticks up and start framing. There is groundwork and foundational work that must first be approved, implemented, and inspected. The plan would be a disastrous failure if one attempted to skip or avoid steps in the building process. Likewise, with scripture memory, you have to create and follow closely a well-thought-out plan.

There are many resources out there offering similar or slightly different ideas and suggestions on how to approach the planning process. These are just the ones that I have tested and proved as effective and reliable. I hope you will consider trying. There are eight steps to the planning process.

1. The first step in the plan is to pick a Bible translation that works best for you and stick with it. This step is not absolutely critical, though I have found it very helpful. I used to dabble in scripture memory in High School after giving my life to Christ. At that time, I had the 1984 Edition New International Version Study Bible. I went through a long season of "not memorizing scripture," but when God placed on my heart to turn that switch back on, I chose the same translation. Not only did I choose the same translation, but I started with verses that I had memorized years prior. This will prove to be very helpful as you start this discipline. Habits, both good ones and bad ones, are hard to break. We want to establish and build upon good techniques to effect positive adaptations and

change. Thus, create good habits. Consider any habit that you want to make routine. You must be disciplined and stick to it over time to create a well-worn path.

2. The second step in the plan is to pick your first verse. As I mentioned earlier, I had at one time memorized a number of Bible verses while in high school. I had since forgotten them, but not entirely. They had simply been stored deep in the attic of my mind, gathering dust. When I relaunched scripture memory, I went through and found verses that I had committed to memory so many years earlier. Starting with verses you already know or are familiar with will help you gain momentum, and that will prove to be motivating. I suggest that you start with a short, single Bible verse. There is no reason to start memorizing scripture with a long, challenging verse. If you have not been to the gym in years and suddenly start back up, it would be painful and foolish to jump on the treadmill and run ten miles at maximum effort. Nobody in their right mind would do that. Instead, they would ease into the training. Likewise,

ease into internalizing the Word of God in your heart. Consider Psalm 119:11 as your first verse, which says, "I have hidden your word in my heart that I might not sin against you." This is the single verse that became the engine behind why I started His Word, My Heart Ministry.

I must reiterate the very first step in internalizing His Word in our hearts is *prayer.* That principle and practice remain paramount and primary throughout your day and life. Remember, this is not rote memorization for the sake of memorization. The purpose is to know each verse thoroughly and completely, taking it from head knowledge and cementing it in your heart. Just like the foundation of a home is built on a thick layer of rebar-reinforced concrete.

3. The third step will bring you back to your days in high school and college. Flash cards! I recommend buying a fresh stack of three-by-five flash cards with lines on only one side. Though this might sound obvious, allow me to explain. On the lined side at the top, clearly print the address of

the verse to be memorized, Psalm 119:11. It is important to note that I am a strong advocate of memorizing the address or the Bible verse reference, the book, the chapter, and the verse. I promise that though this adds another layer of difficulty to scripture memory, it will prove invaluable in your recall and testimony as you share with others exhorting them to the truth. I referenced earlier one of my all-time favorite verses, 1 Peter 4:11, where Peter says, "If anyone speaks, he should do it as one speaking the very words of God." When people see God's light in your life and hope in the midst of trials or tribulations and ask, "Why do we have hope, and where does our hope come from?" when we recite an applicable verse detailing the address, the impact not only glorifies God but gives the one questioning the Bible verse so they can look it up for themselves.

After you write the address at the top of the lined side, then clearly write out the entire verse. Then flip the card over and, in the center of the non-lined side, write out the address again. Then take two more cards and repeat so that you have three identical flash cards. Why three cards? One of the cards is to stay where you keep your Bible and study materials. The second can be placed on the dash of your car (with the lined side out so you can glance at it while in traffic or stopped), or you can place it on the cupboards in your kitchen or mirror in your bathroom. You get the idea. The last card is placed in your pocket. When a free moment presents itself during the day, instead of scrolling through social media, pull out your verse and go over it.

This becomes an amazing evangelical tool to prompt discussions with friends, family, coworkers, or even strangers. Over the years, my stack of flash cards has grown quite large. I often bring them to work and to the gym, and I am frequently asked, "What are you studying?" The unassuming person thinks I am in school, but when I respond, "Oh, these are Bible verses that I am committing to memory." Those who are disinterested quickly regret asking the question and make haste in their departure. However, some people stick around and ask more follow-up questions. This is where we get to plant seeds for the Gospel of Jesus Christ.

4. The fourth step involves downloading the "free" Bible Memory App on your phone. This application is amazing, and I cannot emphasize enough how it has improved and enhanced my capacity to memorize Scripture. The app is free for the first fifty verses, then there's a one-time $10 charge if you want to continue. This is the pro version, which has a lot more features that are incredibly useful. I would suggest that you just download and pay for the Pro version. The enhanced features are game changers. I have created a short tutorial on how to navigate and use this app. In this day and age, almost everyone has a smartphone. Instead of killing time with scrolling social media, open the Bible Memory App and review your Scriptures.

5. The fifth step involves music. There are countless case studies and articles that claim that music can enhance one's capacity to study and memorize. You can simply search "relaxing study music" or something

similar to find a number of different melodies that can help you focus while you practice the steps of scripture memory. It's said that "Music activates both the left and right brain at the same time, and the activation of both hemispheres can maximize learning and improve memory." There's another form of music that will augment your ability to memorize. Consider music that you listen to regularly, no matter the genre. You find a song you really like (hopefully a worship song), and after not too long, you know the melody and the words. There are a number of different songs and music that put a melody to scripture. Some may sound like children's music, but the benefit is for all ages. Seeds Family Music is a ministry that creates scripture memory songs that can be watched and downloaded on almost all of the platforms available.

6. The sixth step to internalizing God's Word involves studying the verse and meditating on it. Remember when God told Joshua, "Do not let this book of the law depart from your mouth; meditate on it day and night…" (Joshua 1:8). The world has com-

pletely distorted and corrupted the practice of meditation. Today, the world defines mediation as emptying your mind. The Bible uses the word mediate with a completely different definition and outcome. It means to fill your mind as you ponder, consider, and contemplate the meaning of the author's original intent of the verse.

Remember, the goal is to internalize and assimilate the Word of God in our heads and hearts. The steps and techniques that I have listed so far may sound like just simple Bible verse memorization. Friends, I am advocating for so much more than that. The purpose is to be transformed by the renewing of our minds by filling our minds with His Word. Letting His Word dwell, live, abide in us richly (Romans 12:1–2 and Colossians 3:16). Remember we are sanctified and made more like Christ through the Word. The meditation process is first initiated when we take time to study the Word.

Ezra 7:10 says this, "Ezra had devoted himself to the study and observance of the Law of the Lord and to teaching its decrees and laws in Israel." Look closely there in that verse. It says that he "studied" and "observed" the law. This technique is paramount when opening the living and active Word of God. Use these three steps, in order, to help you study and grasp the Word to subsequently meditate on. They are observed, interpreted, and then applied.

a. *Observation.* This simply means reading the verse and asking yourself, "What does this verse say?" This is not to be confused with the second step, which is interpretation. In the observation step, you are looking at grammar and punctuation. You are looking at the words used, how often they are repeated, and what words are emphasized. In this step, you can rewrite the verse in your own words. It has been said that 75 percent of your Bible study time ought to be allocated for this step.

b. *Interpretation.* In this step, you get to explore commentaries and see what the biblical scholars say about what the verse actually means. Reference dictionaries, *Interlinear Bibles*, and concordances. This is the step where you get to say to yourself, "What does this verse mean?" In the interpretation step, you get to explore the footnotes that are attached to the verse.

c. *Application.* In this step, we get to put the verse into action. "How does this verse fit into your life?" Practically speaking, we implement the verse(s) into daily lives and prayers. Hebrews 4:12 says, "For the Word of God is living and active. Sharper than any doubled-edged sword, it penetrates even to dividing soul and spirit, joints, and marrow; it judges the thoughts and attitudes of the heart." When we look intently into the word, observe what it says, interpret what it means, and then apply it to our daily lives, it has the ability to cut us and change our lives for His glory forever.

7. The seventh step is short and sweet. If you are on social media, then find and follow people who share memorized or recited scripture. By following accounts that

quote, memorize, recite, or read scripture, it might offer some verses that others have shared that really speak to you. Verses that you may choose to internalize and hide in your heart.

8. The last step involves activating and engaging as many tools and senses as possible to commit the verse(s) to memory. This is practicing and utilizing various techniques. The following is a short list of instructional tips that have helped me internalize God's Word in my heart. Some of these techniques can be combined together to get the biggest bang for your buck.

Read it

This is obvious but must not be overlooked. We talked about "rote memorization," which really starts and stays very cerebral and can often have fleeting results. That is why the emphasis is not on memorization but on internalization. To be truly transformed by the Word, we have to take the head knowledge and usher it deep into our hearts. The hope is that the words of our mouths and the meditation of our hearts would be pleasing to the Lord (Psalm 19:14) and that our mouths would be the conduit for what resides in our hearts. "For out of the overflow of our hearts, the mouth speaks" (Luke 6:45). When you read the verse, try reading it out loud. This will activate two senses at once. Reading effectively out loud is a learned skill that through practice and repetition becomes easier and more fluid.

Write it

This technique involves writing the verse(s) down over and over again. The goal is to write it down completely from memory, but it takes time and practice. My wife practices memorizing scripture, and she likes to take the verse and rewrite it in her own words. First, you take your flash card with the written out facing up. Then you have a blank piece of paper and start writing out your verse. You glance over to quickly look at and reference the verse and continue to write out the verse. A bonus technique to this step is to read it out loud while doing this.

Another technique we will call "Emphasize it." This involves writing and rewriting the verse the number of times that there are words in the verse. Each time you rewrite the verse, you *emphasize* (make bold) the emphasized word in the verse.

You go through the whole verse (while reading it out loud) until that last word of the verse is emphasized. Let me show you an example. Take Romans 12:12. "Be joyful in hope, patient in affliction, and faithful in prayer." Now there are eleven words in that verse, which means you will write it eleven times.

The first rewrite would look like this, "*Be* joyful in hope, patient in affliction."

The second rewrite would be, "Be *Joyful* in hope, patient in affliction."

The third rewrite, "Be joyful *in* hope, patient in affliction."

I think you get the idea. This technique accelerates the internalization process exponentially.

Hear it

This technique can be accomplished in a number of ways. As I just mentioned, when you practice writing out your memory verse, you read it out loud. This will activate another sense, hearing. When we bring all three of these techniques together, it creates a threefold barrier to distractions. It is multitasking with a singular focus. So practice reading and, in this case, reciting your verse out loud. The Bible Memory App has an option for the user to dictate the verse into a microphone that you can then set on repeat and listen to while driving or going on walks; you get the idea. This is meditating on His Word day and night. Listening to your memory verse in your own voice will solidify it in your heart. Another way to utilize the hearing sense is to ask your spouse or a friend to quiz you. Have them read your flashcards, read your verse, and you respond with the address.

Whiteboard it

This method will require a whiteboard. You write out the verse double-spaced with two spaces between each word. The idea is to create space between the verses as you will be randomly erasing one word after each time you recite the entire verse. Let me show you what this will look like. Here's the sequence:

Romans 10:13
For everyone who calls on the
name of the Lord will be saved.

Romans 10:13
For —— who calls of the name
of the Lord will be saved.

Romans 10:13
For —— who calls on the ——
of the Lord will be saved.

Romans 10:13
For —— who calls on the ——
of the —— will be saved.

You can see that with each step, one word is erased from the verse, but you read the entire verse as if all the words were present.

In the last sequence, the whiteboard will be empty, including the address, and you will recite the verse from memory.

Share it

This sounds like more of a reason to memorize and internalize His Word in our hearts rather than a technique for committing it to memory. I say, "It is accomplishing both." There are countless reasons why we ought to share our memory verses with our families, friends, coworkers, and the world.

Let me give one verse by way of explaining why share it. Romans 10:17 says, "Faith comes from hearing the message, and the message is heard through the

Word of Christ." It is God who justifies, saves, rescues, and redeems. We simply get to be participants in the salvation of those He has called. In Ephesians 2:10, Paul encourages the Saints, saying, "For we are God's workmanship created in Christ Jesus to do good works which God has prepared in advance for us to do." What an amazing privilege it is that we get to partner with the Lord in his redemptive plan.

Sharing your memory verses while they are curing and being cemented in your heart shows vulnerability and humility to hearers. We have all seen the caution tape that is erected around a not-yet-cured driveway, sidewalk, or foundation. The cement has not yet become concrete. Cement and water are the ingredients that form concrete. When they are mixed together, a chemical reaction takes place, initiating the launch sequence to form concrete. When we see cement curing, we do not doubt for a second that in a few hours, the mushy mess will soon become rock-hard, impenetrable concrete. They say it takes twenty-eight days for concrete to fully cure. That is a long time. Similarly, it takes a long time to memorize scripture. It is a spiritual discipline that takes practice, daily practice. This principle is applied to almost everything. If your goal is to gain muscle in the gym, it is not going to happen if you work out only once with no pattern of consistency or discipline.

You do not have to wait until your verse or verses are cured. Sharing the wet cement demonstrates that we value God's Word enough to possibly become embarrassed as we fumble through the verse(s). It is exposing our hearts. Paul talks about not being ashamed of the Gospel in Romans 1:16 because it is the power of God for the salvation of everyone who believes, and in Philippians 1:20, he said, "I eagerly expect and hope that I will in no way be ashamed but will have sufficient courage so that Christ will be exalted in his life." Whether we successfully share the memory verse wholly without stuttering, recalling the address and everything, or if we mess up the verse and forget the address, God is glorified in our effort. Both motivate us to stay locked in and engaged in spiritual discipline.

These eight steps to memorizing and internalizing the Word of God in your heart are going to take discipline and objective effort. There is one more thing that I would like to talk about. You have likely seen and heard others advocating for the memorization of whole chapters and books. This is a high-level goal and one that I personally aspire to do. However, it takes a lot of time to accomplish and maintain.

That is to say that it is well worth the effort, just like memorizing single verses or smaller sections in the Word. I have found that when I recite sections of scripture longer than about five or so verses, the hearers begin to focus more on how I am able to recite rather than what I am saying. When I am finished, they will often times ask how I was able to memorize such long sections instead of being encouraged or exhorted through the verses. My goal and purpose in sharing memorized scripture is to exhort, encourage, and equip. I want Christians to hear the very words of God and subsequently desire to hide His Word in their hearts. Nevertheless, if you are just starting out, I would recommend starting with one or two verses, but be sure to know and understand the context.

Step 4: Go Do It

Is it going to be difficult? Yes. But it will unequivocally, without a shred or shadow of doubt, change your life. It has changed my life, and I sincerely desire that for you, too.

Final Thoughts

Internalizing God's Word in our hearts has a far greater reward in your life than receiving $1000 for each verse. The lasting effect compounds exponentially beyond what we can ask or imagine. Chuck Swindoll said this about memorizing Scripture:

I know of no other single practice in the Christian life that's more rewarding, practically speaking, than memorizing Scripture. That's right. No other single discipline is more useful and rewarding than this. No other single exercise pays greater spiritual dividends! Your prayer life will be strengthened. Your witnessing will be sharper and much more effective. Your counseling will be in demand. Your attitude and outlook will begin to change. Your mind will become alert and observant. Your confidence and assurance will be enhanced. Your faith will be solidified.

Please check out and share my YouTube channel all for the Glory of God and propagation of the Gospel: https://youtu.be/CK99gHr4OvM.

ABOUT THE AUTHOR

Mike Harrison was introduced to the Gospel when he was fifteen years old. He was invited to Sonshine Ministries, a Christian summer camp, where he learned how to water ski and was introduced to Jesus Christ.

In the summer of 1989, he accepted the Lord into his life. Later in high school, he was introduced to firefighting as a profession and spent nearly twenty-seven years as a firefighter. In 1998, he married his beautiful wife, of now twenty-six years, raising two amazing college-age children. His career was cut short due to a work injury causing him to retire from the Santa Rosa Fire Department in the spring of 2022.

During the injury period, the Lord placed scripture memory in his heart. In Romans 12:9–10, Paul pleaded with God to take away the "thorn in his flesh," and God so lovingly and graciously responded, "My grace is sufficient for you, for my power is made perfect in your weakness." These verses and many others have encouraged Mike to trust in the Lord with all his heart.

His passion for the Word has not slowed down ever since. It has only increased, prompting him to teach, train, and disciple others who want to experience intimacy with God through internalizing His Word.

In January of 2024, God called him into ministry. Mike accepted the pastor position at Deerfield Community Church in Truckee, California. He continues to work full-time as the manager for High

Sierra Custom Door while shepherding the Lord's church in Truckee.

If you're ever in Truckee, come check out Deerfield Community Church.

Printed in the USA
CPSIA information can be obtained
at www.ICGtesting.com
LVHW091808051024
792969LV00003B/606